CONTENTS

page 8

page 14

page 26

page 44

HOISIN SRIRACHA CHICKEN WINGS

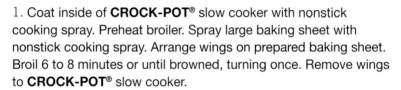

3 pounds chicken wings, tips removed and split at joints

½ cup hoisin sauce

¼ cup plus 1 tablespoon sriracha sauce, divided

2 tablespoons packed brown sugar

Chopped green onions (optional)

1. Coat inside of **CROCK-POT®** slow cooker with nonstick cooking spray. Preheat broiler. Spray large baking sheet with nonstick cooking spray. Arrange wings on prepared baking sheet. Broil 6 to 8 minutes or until browned, turning once. Remove wings to **CROCK-POT®** slow cooker.

2. Combine hoisin sauce, ¼ cup sriracha sauce and brown sugar in medium bowl; stir to blend. Pour sauce mixture over wings in **CROCK-POT®** slow cooker; stir to coat. Cover; cook on LOW 3½ to 4 hours. Remove wings to large serving platter; cover with foil to keep warm.

3. Turn **CROCK-POT®** slow cooker to HIGH. Cook, uncovered, on HIGH 10 to 15 minutes or until sauce is thickened. Stir in remaining 1 tablespoon sriracha sauce. Spoon sauce over wings to serve. Garnish with green onions.

Makes 5 to 6 servings

PINEAPPLE AND PORK TERIYAKI

Nonstick cooking spray
2 pork tenderloins (1¼ pounds *each*)
1 can (8 ounces) pineapple chunks
½ cup teriyaki sauce
3 tablespoons honey
1 tablespoon minced fresh ginger

1. Spray large skillet with cooking spray; heat over medium-high heat. Add pork; cook 8 minutes or until browned on all sides. Remove to oval-shaped **CROCK-POT®** slow cooker.

2. Combine pineapple, teriyaki sauce, honey and ginger in large bowl; stir to blend. Pour over pork. Cover; cook on LOW 6 to 7 hours or on HIGH 3 to 4 hours. Remove pork to large cutting board; cover loosely with foil. Let stand 15 minutes before slicing.

3. Cover; cook on HIGH 10 to 15 minutes or until sauce is thickened. Serve sliced pork with pineapple and cooking liquid.

Makes 6 to 8 servings

ASIAN BEEF WITH BROCCOLI

 1 boneless beef chuck roast (about 1½ pounds),
    sliced into thin strips*

 1 can (about 14 ounces) condensed beef broth,
    undiluted

 ½ cup oyster sauce

 2 tablespoons cornstarch

 1 bag (16 ounces) fresh broccoli florets

    Hot cooked rice

    Sesame seeds (optional)

Freeze steak 30 minutes to make slicing easier.

1. Place beef in **CROCK-POT®** slow cooker. Pour broth and oyster sauce over beef. Cover; cook on HIGH 3 hours.

2. Stir 2 tablespoons cooking liquid into cornstarch in small bowl until smooth; whisk into **CROCK-POT®** slow cooker. Cover; cook on HIGH 15 minutes or until thickened.

3. Cook broccoli according to package directions. Add to **CROCK-POT®** slow cooker; toss gently to mix. Serve with rice. Garnish with sesame seeds.

Makes 4 to 6 servings

MU SHU TURKEY

- 1 can (16 ounces) plums, drained and pitted
- ½ cup orange juice
- ¼ cup finely chopped onion
- 1 tablespoon minced fresh ginger
- ¼ teaspoon ground cinnamon
- 1 pound boneless, skinless turkey breast, cut into thin strips
- 6 (7-inch) flour tortillas, warmed
- 3 cups coleslaw mix

Orange wedges (optional)

1. Place plums in blender or food processor; blend until almost smooth. Combine plums, orange juice, onion, ginger and cinnamon in **CROCK-POT®** slow cooker; mix well. Place turkey over plum mixture. Cover; cook on LOW 3 to 4 hours.

2. Divide turkey evenly among tortillas. Spoon 2 tablespoons plum sauce over turkey; top with ½ cup coleslaw mix. Fold up bottom edges of tortillas over filling, fold in sides and roll up to enclose filling. Serve with remaining plum sauce and orange wedges, if desired.

Makes 6 servings

Tip: To thicken a sauce in the **CROCK-POT®** slow cooker, remove the solid foods using a slotted spoon and reserve sauce in the **CROCK-POT®** slow cooker. Mix ¼ cup cold water into 1 to 2 tablespoons cornstarch in small bowl until smooth; whisk into the sauce. Cover; cook on HIGH 15 minutes or until sauce is thickened.

SPICY ORANGE CHICKEN NUGGETS

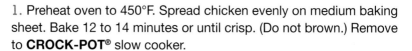

    1   bag (28 ounces) frozen popcorn chicken bites
 1½   cups prepared honey teriyaki marinade
    ¾   cup orange juice concentrate
    ⅔   cup water
    1   tablespoon orange marmalade
    ½   teaspoon hot chile sauce or sriracha*
        Thinly sliced green onions (optional)
        Hot cooked rice

1. Preheat oven to 450°F. Spread chicken evenly on medium baking sheet. Bake 12 to 14 minutes or until crisp. (Do not brown.) Remove to **CROCK-POT®** slow cooker.

2. Combine teriyaki marinade, juice concentrate, water, marmalade and chile sauce in medium bowl; stir to blend. Pour over chicken. Cover; cook on LOW 3 to 3½ hours.

3. Sprinkle with green onions, if desired, and serve with rice.

Makes 8 to 9 servings

MEDITERRANEAN BEAN SOUP WITH ORZO AND FETA

2 cans (about 14 ounces *each*) vegetable broth

1 can (about 14 ounces) Italian-style diced tomatoes

1 package (10 ounces) frozen mixed carrots and peas

½ cup uncooked orzo pasta

2 teaspoons dried oregano

1 can (about 15 ounces) chickpeas, rinsed and drained

½ cup crumbled feta cheese (optional)

1. Coat inside of **CROCK-POT**® slow cooker with nonstick cooking spray. Combine broth, tomatoes, carrots and peas, pasta and oregano in **CROCK-POT**® slow cooker.

2. Cover; cook on LOW 5 to 6 hours or on HIGH 2 to 3 hours. Stir in chickpeas. Cover; cook on HIGH 10 minutes or until heated through. Top each serving with cheese, if desired.

Makes 6 servings

JAMAICAN QUINOA AND SWEET POTATO STEW

3 cups vegetable broth

1 large *or* 2 small sweet potatoes (12 ounces), cut into ¾-inch pieces

1 cup uncooked quinoa, rinsed and drained

1 large red bell pepper, cut into ¾-inch pieces

1 tablespoon Caribbean jerk seasoning

¼ cup chopped fresh cilantro

¼ cup sliced almonds, toasted*

Hot pepper sauce or Pickapeppa sauce (optional)

To toast almonds, spread in single layer in heavy skillet. Cook and stir over medium heat 1 to 2 minutes or until nuts are lightly browned.

1. Coat inside of **CROCK-POT®** slow cooker with nonstick cooking spray. Combine broth, potatoes, quinoa, bell pepper and jerk seasoning in **CROCK-POT®** slow cooker; stir to blend. Cover; cook on LOW 5 to 6 hours or on HIGH 2 to 2½ hours.

2. Top each serving with cilantro and almonds. Serve with hot pepper sauce, if desired.

Makes 4 servings

BLACK AND WHITE CHILI

Nonstick cooking spray

1 pound chicken tenders, cut into ¾-inch pieces

1 cup coarsely chopped onion

1 can (about 15 ounces) Great Northern beans, rinsed and drained

1 can (about 15 ounces) black beans, rinsed and drained

1 can (about 14 ounces) Mexican-style stewed tomatoes, undrained

2 tablespoons Texas-style chili powder seasoning mix

1. Spray large skillet with cooking spray; heat over medium heat. Add chicken and onion; cook and stir 5 minutes or until chicken is browned.

2. Combine chicken mixture, beans, tomatoes and chili seasoning in **CROCK-POT®** slow cooker; stir to blend. Cover; cook on LOW 4 to 4½ hours.

Makes 6 servings

Serving Suggestion: For a change of pace, serve this delicious chili over cooked rice or pasta.

CARAMELIZED FRENCH ONION SOUP

4   extra-large sweet onions, peeled

¼   cup (½ stick) butter

2   cups dry white wine

8   cups beef or vegetable broth, divided

2   cups water

1   tablespoon minced fresh thyme

6   slices French bread, toasted

1   cup (4 ounces) shredded Swiss or Gruyère cheese

1. Cut each onion into quarters. Cut each quarter into ¼-inch-thick slices. Heat large skillet over medium heat. Add butter and onions; cook 45 to 50 minutes or until soft and caramel brown, stirring occasionally. Remove to **CROCK-POT®** slow cooker.

2. Add wine to skillet; simmer 15 minutes or until liquid is reduced to about ½ cup. Remove to **CROCK-POT®** slow cooker.

3. Add broth, water and thyme to **CROCK-POT®** slow cooker. Cover; cook on HIGH 2½ hours.

4. To serve, ladle soup into individual ovenproof soup bowls. Float 1 slice of toast in each bowl and sprinkle with cheese. Preheat broiler. Broil 3 to 5 minutes or until cheese is melted and golden.

Makes 6 servings

EASY BEEF STEW

1½ to 2 pounds cubed beef stew meat

4 medium potatoes, cubed

4 carrots, cut into 1½-inch pieces *or* 4 cups baby carrots

1 medium onion, cut into 8 slices

2 cans (8 ounces *each*) tomato sauce

1 teaspoon salt

½ teaspoon black pepper

Combine beef, potatoes, carrots, onion, tomato sauce, salt and pepper in **CROCK-POT®** slow cooker; stir to blend. Cover; cook on LOW 8 to 10 hours.

Makes 6 to 8 servings

PORK TENDERLOIN CHILI

1½ to 2 pounds pork tenderloin, cooked and cut into 2-inch pieces

2 cans (about 15 ounces *each*) pinto beans, rinsed and drained

2 cans (about 15 ounces *each*) black beans, rinsed and drained

2 cans (about 14 ounces *each*) whole tomatoes

2 cans (4 ounces *each*) diced mild green chiles

1 package taco seasoning mix

Optional toppings: diced avocado, shredded cheese, chopped onion, fresh chopped cilantro and/or tortilla chips

Combine pork, beans, tomatoes, chiles and taco seasoning mix in **CROCK-POT®** slow cooker; stir to blend. Cover; cook on LOW 4 hours. Top as desired.

Makes 8 servings

SOUPS, STEWS AND CHILIES

EASY BEEF STEW

BEEFY TOSTADA PIE

2 teaspoons olive oil

1½ cups chopped onion

2 pounds ground beef

1 teaspoon salt

1 teaspoon ground cumin

1 teaspoon chili powder

2 cloves garlic, minced

1 can (15 ounces) tomato sauce

1 cup sliced black olives

8 (6-inch) flour tortillas

3½ cups (16 ounces) shredded Cheddar cheese

Sour cream, salsa and chopped green onion (optional)

1. Heat oil in large skillet over medium heat. Add onion; cook and stir 3 to 5 minutes or until tender. Add beef, salt, cumin and chili powder; cook and stir 6 to 8 minutes or until beef is browned. Drain fat. Stir in tomato sauce; cook until heated through. Stir in olives.

2. Make foil handles using three 18×2-inch strips of heavy-duty foil or use regular foil folded to double thickness. Crisscross foil in spoke design; place across bottom and up side of **CROCK-POT®** slow cooker. Lay 1 tortilla on foil strips. Spread with meat sauce and ½ cup cheese. Top with another tortilla, meat sauce and cheese. Repeat layers five times, ending with tortilla. Cover; cook on HIGH 1½ hours.

3. To serve, lift out of **CROCK-POT®** slow cooker using foil handles and remove to large serving platter. Discard foil. Cut into wedges. Serve with sour cream, salsa and green onion, if desired.

Makes 4 to 6 servings

MEXICAN CARNITAS

  1 boneless pork shoulder roast (2 pounds)
  1 tablespoon garlic salt
  1 tablespoon black pepper
1½ teaspoons adobo seasoning
  1 medium onion, chopped
  1 can (16 ounces) green salsa
 ½ cup water
 ¼ cup chopped fresh cilantro
     Juice of 2 medium limes
  3 cloves garlic, minced
  4 (6-inch) flour tortillas, warmed
     Optional toppings: chopped green bell pepper,
        tomatoes and red onion
     Lime wedges (optional)

1. Coat inside of **CROCK-POT®** slow cooker with nonstick cooking spray. Season pork with garlic salt, black pepper and adobo seasoning.

2. Place pork, onion, salsa, water, cilantro, lime juice and garlic in **CROCK-POT®** slow cooker. Cover; cook on LOW 4 to 5 hours. Serve in tortillas with desired toppings. Garnish with lime wedges.

Makes 4 servings

BLACK BEAN AND MUSHROOM CHILAQUILES

- 2 tablespoons olive oil
- 1 medium onion, chopped
- 1 medium green bell pepper, chopped
- 1 jalapeño or serrano pepper, seeded and minced*
- 2 cans (about 15 ounces *each*) black beans, rinsed and drained
- 1 can (about 14 ounces) diced tomatoes
- 10 ounces white mushrooms, cut into quarters
- 1½ teaspoons ground cumin
- 1½ teaspoons dried oregano
- 1 cup (4 ounces) shredded sharp white Cheddar cheese, plus additional for garnish
- 6 cups baked tortilla chips

Jalapeño and serrano peppers can sting and irritate the skin, so wear rubber gloves when handling peppers and do not touch your eyes.

1. Heat oil in medium skillet over medium heat. Add onion, bell pepper and jalapeño pepper; cook and stir 5 minutes or until onion is softened. Remove to **CROCK-POT®** slow cooker. Add beans, tomatoes, mushrooms, cumin and oregano. Cover; cook on LOW 6 hours or on HIGH 3 hours.

2. Sprinkle 1 cup Cheddar cheese over beans and mushrooms. Cover; cook on HIGH 15 minutes or until cheese is melted. Stir to combine.

3. For each serving, coarsely crush 1 cup tortilla chips into individual serving bowls. Top with black bean mixture. Garnish with additional cheese.

Makes 6 servings

LAYERED MEXICAN-STYLE CASSEROLE

2 cans (about 15 ounces *each*) hominy, drained

1 can (about 15 ounces) black beans, rinsed and drained

1 can (about 14 ounces) diced tomatoes with garlic, basil and oregano

1 cup thick and chunky salsa

1 can (6 ounces) tomato paste

½ teaspoon ground cumin

3 (9-inch) flour tortillas

2 cups (8 ounces) shredded Monterey Jack cheese

¼ cup sliced black olives

1. Prepare foil handles (see Note). Coat inside of **CROCK-POT®** slow cooker with nonstick cooking spray. Combine hominy, beans, tomatoes, salsa, tomato paste and cumin in large bowl; stir to blend.

2. Press 1 tortilla in bottom of **CROCK-POT®** slow cooker. Top with one third of hominy mixture and one third of cheese. Repeat layers. Press remaining tortilla on top. Top with remaining hominy mixture. Set aside remaining one third of cheese.

3. Cover; cook on LOW 6 to 8 hours or on HIGH 2 to 3 hours. Turn off heat. Sprinkle with remaining cheese and olives. Cover; let stand 5 minutes. Pull out tortilla stack with foil handles. Cut into six wedges.

Makes 6 servings

Note: To make foil handles, tear off three 18×2-inch strips of heavy-duty foil or use regular foil folded to double thickness. Crisscross foil strips in spoke design and place in **CROCK-POT®** slow cooker to make lifting of tortilla stack easier.

SHREDDED CHICKEN TACOS

2	pounds boneless, skinless chicken thighs
½	cup prepared mango salsa, plus additional for serving
8	(6-inch) yellow corn tortillas, warmed
	Optional toppings: shredded pepper jack cheese, sour cream and/or lettuce

1. Coat inside of **CROCK-POT®** slow cooker with nonstick cooking spray. Add chicken and ½ cup salsa. Cover; cook on LOW 4 to 5 hours or on HIGH 2½ to 3 hours.

2. Remove chicken to large cutting board; shred with two forks. Serve shredded chicken in tortillas. Top as desired.

Makes 4 servings

MEXICAN MEAT LOAF

2	pounds ground beef
2	cups crushed corn chips
1	cup (4 ounces) shredded Cheddar cheese
⅔	cup salsa
2	eggs, beaten
¼	cup taco seasoning mix

Combine beef, chips, cheese, salsa, eggs and taco seasoning mix in large bowl; mix well. Shape meat mixture into loaf and place in **CROCK-POT®** slow cooker. Cover; cook on LOW 8 to 10 hours.

Makes 4 to 6 servings

Tip: To glaze meat loaf, mix together ½ cup ketchup, 2 tablespoons packed brown sugar and 1 teaspoon dry mustard. Spread over the cooked meat loaf. Cover; cook on HIGH 15 minutes.

SHREDDED CHICKEN TACOS

BLACK BEAN, ZUCCHINI AND CORN ENCHILADAS

1	tablespoon vegetable oil
1	medium onion, chopped
2	medium zucchini
2	cups corn
1	large red bell pepper, chopped
1	teaspoon minced garlic
½	teaspoon salt
½	teaspoon ground cumin
¼	teaspoon ground coriander
1	can (about 14 ounces) black beans, rinsed and drained
2	jars (16 ounces *each*) salsa verde
12	(6-inch) corn tortillas
2½	cups shredded Monterey Jack cheese
2	tablespoons chopped fresh cilantro

1. Heat oil in large skillet over medium heat. Add onion; cook 6 minutes or until softened. Add zucchini, corn and bell pepper; cook 2 minutes. Add garlic, salt, cumin and coriander; cook and stir 1 minute. Stir in beans. Remove from heat.

2. Pour 1 cup salsa in bottom of **CROCK-POT®** slow cooker. Arrange 3 tortillas in single layer, cutting the tortillas in half as needed to make them fit. Place 2 cups vegetable mixture over tortillas; sprinkle with ½ cup cheese. Repeat layering two more times. Layer with remaining 3 tortillas; top with 2 cups salsa. Sprinkle with remaining 1 cup cheese. Reserve remaining filling for another use.

3. Cover; cook on HIGH 2 hours or until cheese is bubbly and edges are lightly browned. Sprinkle with cilantro. Let stand 10 minutes before serving.

Makes 6 servings

TRIPLE CHOCOLATE FANTASY

2 pounds white almond bark, broken into pieces

1 bar (4 ounces) sweetened chocolate, broken into pieces*

1 package (12 ounces) semisweet chocolate chips

3 cups coarsely chopped pecans, toasted**

*Use your favorite high-quality chocolate candy bar.

**To toast pecans, spread in single layer in heavy skillet. Cook and stir over medium heat 1 to 2 minutes or until nuts are lightly browned.

1. Place bark, sweetened chocolate and chocolate chips in **CROCK-POT®** slow cooker. Cover; cook on HIGH 1 hour. Do not stir.

2. Turn **CROCK-POT®** slow cooker to LOW. Cover; cook on LOW 1 hour, stirring every 15 minutes. Stir in nuts.

3. Drop mixture by tablespoonfuls onto baking sheet covered with waxed paper; cool. Store in tightly covered container.

Makes 36 pieces

Variations: Here are a few ideas for other imaginative items to add in along with or instead of the pecans: raisins, crushed peppermint candy, candy-coated baking bits, crushed toffee, peanuts or pistachio nuts, chopped gum drops, chopped dried fruit, candied cherries, chopped marshmallows or sweetened coconut.

FRESH BOSC PEAR GRANITA

1   pound fresh Bosc pears, peeled, cored and cubed

1¼   cups water

¼   cup sugar

½   teaspoon ground cinnamon

1   tablespoon lemon juice

Fresh raspberries (optional)

Lemon slices (optional)

Fresh mint leaves (optional)

1. Place pears, water, sugar and cinnamon in **CROCK-POT®** slow cooker. Cover; cook on HIGH 2½ to 3½ hours or until pears are very soft and tender. Stir in lemon juice.

2. Remove pears and syrup to blender or food processor; blend until smooth. Strain mixture, discarding any pulp. Pour liquid into 13×9-inch baking pan. Cover tightly with plastic wrap. Place pan in freezer.

3. Stir every hour, tossing granita with fork. Crush any lumps in mixture as it freezes. Freeze 3 to 4 hours or until firm. You may keep granita in freezer up to two days before serving; toss granita every 6 to 12 hours. Garnish with raspberries, lemon slices and mint.

Makes 6 servings

WARM HONEY LEMONADE

4½ cups water

2½ cups lemon juice

1 cup orange juice

1 cup honey

¼ cup sugar

Lemon slices (optional)

Combine water, lemon juice, orange juice, honey and sugar in
CROCK-POT® slow cooker; whisk well. Cover; cook on LOW
2 hours. Whisk well. Turn **CROCK-POT®** slow cooker to WARM
setting to serve. Garnish with lemon slices.

Makes 9 cups

FIGS POACHED IN RED WINE

2 cups dry red wine

1 cup packed brown sugar

12 dried Calimyrna or Mediterranean figs
(about 6 ounces)

2 (3-inch) cinnamon sticks

1 teaspoon finely grated orange peel

4 tablespoons whipping cream (optional)

1. Combine wine, brown sugar, figs, cinnamon sticks and orange
peel in **CROCK-POT®** slow cooker. Cover; cook on LOW 5 to
6 hours or on HIGH 4 to 5 hours.

2. Remove and discard cinnamon sticks. To serve, spoon figs and
syrup into serving dish. Top with cream, if desired.

Makes 4 servings

WARM HONEY LEMONADE

TEQUILA-POACHED PEARS

- 4 Anjou pears, peeled
- 2 cups water
- 1 can (11½ ounces) pear nectar
- 1 cup tequila
- ½ cup sugar

  Grated peel and juice of 1 lime

  Vanilla ice cream (optional)

1. Place pears in **CROCK-POT®** slow cooker. Combine water, nectar, tequila, sugar, lime peel and lime juice in medium saucepan. Bring to a boil over medium-high heat, stirring frequently. Boil 1 minute; pour over pears.

2. Cover; cook on LOW 4 to 6 hours or on HIGH 2 to 3 hours. Serve warm with poaching liquid and vanilla ice cream, if desired.

Makes 4 servings

Tip: Poaching fruit in a sugar, juice or alcohol syrup helps the fruit retain its shape and become more flavorful.

CHERRY DELIGHT

- 1 can (21 ounces) cherry pie filling
- 1 package (about 18 ounces) yellow cake mix
- ½ cup (1 stick) butter, melted
- ⅓ cup chopped walnuts

Place pie filling in **CROCK-POT®** slow cooker. Combine cake mix and butter in medium bowl. Spread evenly over pie filling. Sprinkle with walnuts. Cover; cook on LOW 3 to 4 hours or on HIGH 1½ to 2 hours.

Makes 8 to 10 servings

TEQUILA-POACHED PEARS

FIVE-SPICE APPLE CRISP

1 tablespoon unsalted butter, melted

6 Golden Delicious apples, peeled, cored and cut into ½-inch-thick slices

¼ cup packed light brown sugar

2 teaspoons lemon juice

¾ teaspoon Chinese five-spice powder *or* ½ teaspoon ground cinnamon and ¼ teaspoon ground allspice*

1 cup coarsely crushed almond biscotti

Whipped cream (optional)

Ground nutmeg (optional)

Chinese five-spice powder is a blend of cinnamon, cloves, fennel seed, anise and Szechuan peppercorns. It is available in most supermarkets and at Asian grocery stores.

1. Coat inside of 5-quart **CROCK-POT®** slow cooker with butter. Add apples, brown sugar, lemon juice and five-spice powder; toss to combine.

2. Cover; cook on LOW 3½ hours or until apples are tender. Sprinkle with cookies. Spoon evenly into bowls. Garnish with whipped cream and nutmeg.

Makes 6 servings

SPICED VANILLA APPLESAUCE

5   pounds (about 10 medium) sweet apples
    (such as Fuji or Gala), peeled and cut into
    1-inch pieces

½   cup water

2   teaspoons vanilla

1   teaspoon ground cinnamon

¼   teaspoon grated nutmeg

¼   teaspoon ground cloves

1. Combine apples, water, vanilla, cinnamon, nutmeg and cloves in **CROCK-POT®** slow cooker; stir to blend. Cover; cook on HIGH 3 to 4 hours or until apples are very tender.

2. Turn off heat. Mash mixture with potato masher to smooth out any large lumps. Let cool completely before serving.

Makes 6 cups

46